DEBATING THE ISSUES

Homework

Anika Fajardo

MEDIA ENHANCED BOOKS
AV2 BY WEIGL
ADDED VALUE • AUDIO VISUAL

www.av2books.com

Published by AV^2 by Weigl
350 5th Avenue, 59th Floor New York, NY 10118
Website: www.av2books.com

Library of Congress Cataloging-in-Publication Data

Names: Fajardo, Anika, author.
Title: Homework / Anika Fajardo.
Other titles: Debate about homework
Description: New York, NY : AV2 by Weigl, [2019] | Series: Debating the issues | Audience: Grades 7-8. | Revision of: The debate about homework. | Includes index.
Identifiers: LCCN 2018053442 (print) | LCCN 2018059313 (ebook) | ISBN 9781489696038 (Multi User Ebook) | ISBN 9781489695987 (Single User Ebook) | ISBN 9781489695956 (hardcover :alk. paper) | ISBN 9781489695963(softcover :alk. paper)
Subjects: LCSH: Homework--Juvenile literature.
Classification: LCC LB1048 (ebook) | LCC LB1048 .F39 2019 (print) | DDC 371.30281--dc23
LC record available at https://lccn.loc.gov/2018053442

Printed in the United States of America in Brainerd, Minnesota
1 2 3 4 5 6 7 8 9 0 22 21 20 19 18

122018
112318

First published by North Star in 2018

Project Coordinator: Priyanka Das   Designer: Ana María Vidal

Weigl acknowledges Getty Images, iStock, Shutterstock, and Alamy as its primary image suppliers for this title.

Homework

Contents

The History of Homework 4
Timeline 7

PROS

Homework Helps Students Earn Higher Grades 8
Homework Makes Students Better Learners 14
Homework Is Good for the Brain 20

CONS

Homework Leads to Unhealthy Stress 26
Homework Does Not Make Students Smarter 32
Homework Limits Students' Other Interests 38

Pros and Cons Summary 43
Homework Map 44
Quiz 46
Key Words/Index 47
Log on to www.av2books.com 48

In past centuries, students completed homework on blackboard slates. In some parts of the world, they still do.

The History of Homework

Homework can take many forms. It might involve a worksheet with math problems, or it could be a 10-page research paper. Sometimes, homework is frustrating. Other times, it can be a fun project with friends.

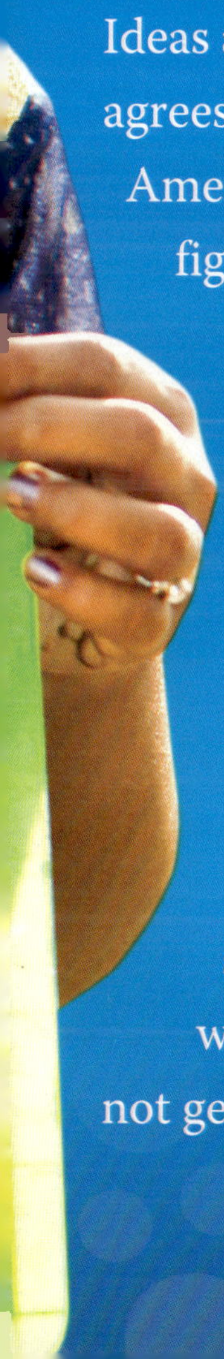

Ideas about homework have changed with time. Not everyone agrees whether homework is a good thing. In the 1800s, American educators wanted children to memorize facts and figures. That meant kids got a lot of homework. In the early 1900s, researcher John Dewey created a new theory. He thought children should practice critical thinking instead of memorizing facts.

Many educators agreed with Dewey. Some thought homework was bad for children. In their opinion, too much time spent on homework caused eye strain and tiredness. Instead, students needed more outdoor activity. Views changed when the Soviet Union launched the first satellite in 1957. Americans worried that the United States was falling behind other nations. They worried students were not getting enough homework.

By the 1980s, reports showed that the United States was far behind other countries in student achievement, especially in math and science. Throughout the 1990s, U.S. teachers started to assign more homework. Students were given homework at a younger age, too. Between 1981 and 2002, the weekly time students spent studying increased by almost one and a half hours.

In the early 2000s, the U.S. Congress created a new law that supported **standardized testing**. More testing meant more homework. When the law was replaced in 2015, homework became an important topic of debate once more.

Homework Amounts

Students around the world are assigned homework by their teachers. In some countries, students are expected to spend several hours completing homework each week. Other countries do not emphasize homework as much.

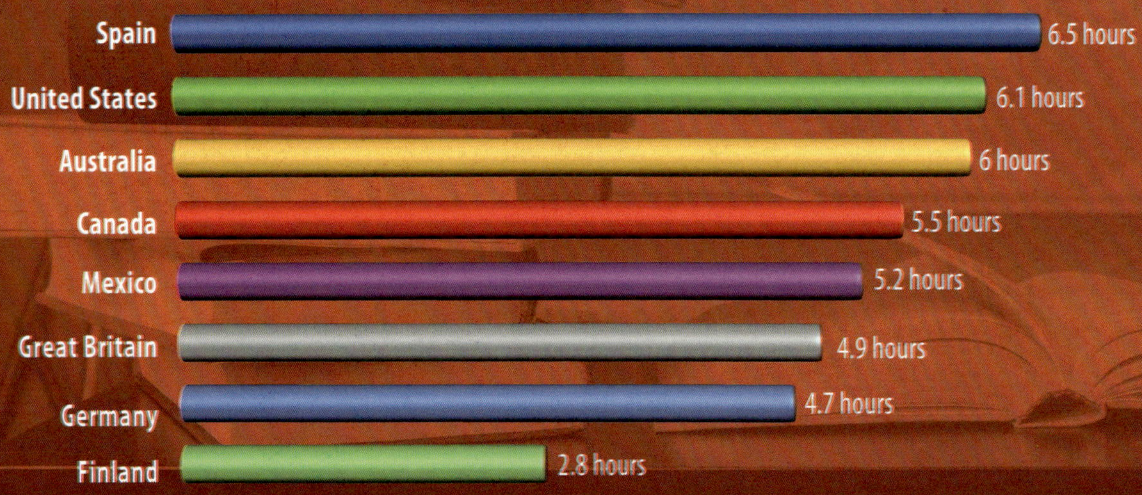

Hours students spend on homework per week (2014)

Timeline

1897

Joseph Mayer Rice, a pediatrician in New York, argues that "mechanical" homework is harmful to children's health.

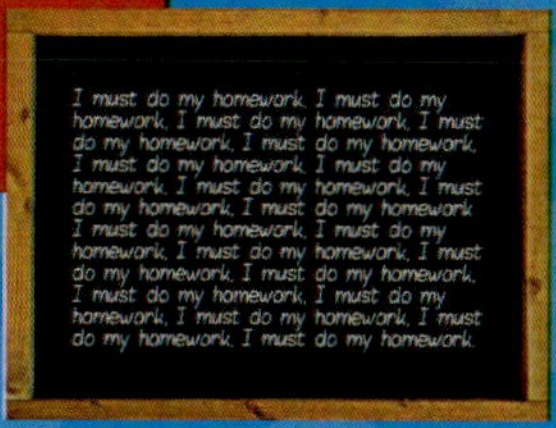

1930

U.S. professor James B. Nash publishes a research summary in which he calls homework "legalized criminality."

1957

The Soviet Union launches the *Sputnik 1* satellite. The United States is concerned about losing the **Cold War**, and the pro-homework movement gains support.

1983

The U.S. government publishes *A Nation at Risk*. This report raises concerns about mediocre performance in schools and calls for an increase in homework.

2000

Students take the first international **PISA** test. Finland, which assigns less homework than the United States, receives higher scores than any other Western country.

2018

Most U.S. students are assigned internet-based homework. This has caused a "Homework Gap," because students in five million households do not have internet at home.

PRO

Students' homework often counts toward their final class grade.

Homework Helps Students Earn Higher Grades

Those in favor of homework argue that work outside of class can help students do better in class. In fact, many studies show a **correlation** between homework and **academic** success. When students regularly spend a reasonable amount of time on homework, their grades increase. Many educators recommend an average of 10 minutes per night per grade level.

In one study, researchers gave a group of students required homework. They gave another group non-required homework. Students in both groups received the same lessons and assignments. But only the students in the first group had to turn in their assignments. At the end of the study, the group with required homework performed better in the class. Researchers theorized that the students with non-required homework were less motivated to study outside of class. That meant they did not perform as well as students with required homework.

Tests can be less intimidating when students do their homework.

Another study showed that required homework makes it harder for students to **procrastinate**. The researchers saw that students with non-required homework sometimes chose to wait until the last minute to study for the test. The students who had required homework, however, were forced to learn the subject little by little. This improved their grades.

Did You Know?

Math is the most commonly assigned homework. A 2013 study showed that 70 percent of students in Grades 3 to 12 had at least one math assignment per week.

Homework Across Grade Levels

The National Parent Teacher Association in the United States recommends giving Grade 1 students no more than 10 to 20 minutes of daily homework. Students in higher grades can be asked to complete an additional 10 minutes per grade.

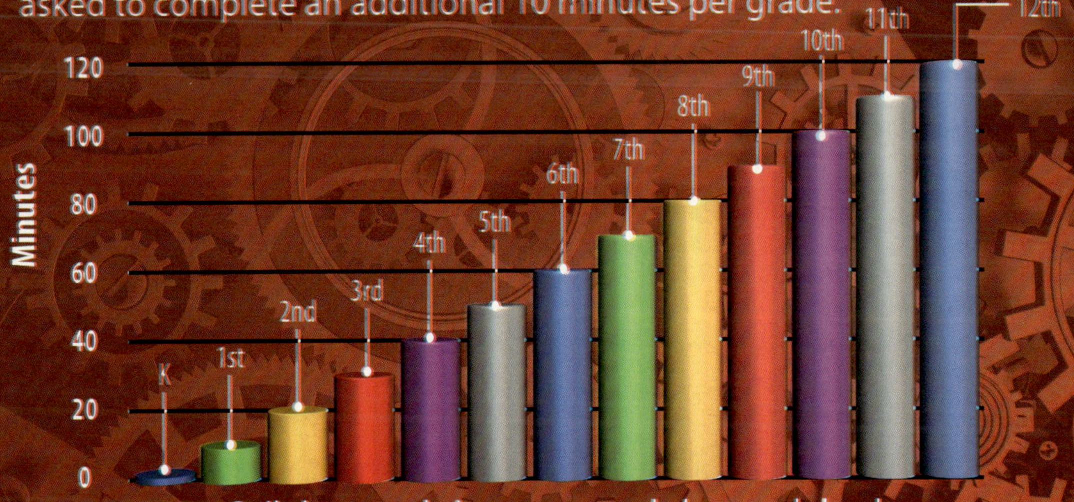

Daily homework time recommended per grade level
(per the National Parent Teacher Association)

Homework is also helpful in subjects that require memorization or practice, such as math. A worksheet filled with math problems gives students an opportunity to practice specific skills. With time, practice helps the students improve their grades.

Homework is also helpful when problems similar to those in the homework appear on the tests. Students who complete the homework are better prepared for exams. As a result, they are more likely to receive higher scores.

Young students often rely on adult guidance when completing their homework.

Homework can also help students do better in school by preparing them for the school day. For example, teachers might ask students to read a chapter for a lesson ahead of time. This will help the students better understand the material when it is introduced in class.

When teachers assign homework—and when students complete it—students do better in school. Sometimes teachers motivate students to complete homework by offering rewards, such as pizza parties or extra recess. They might also have students keep track of their accomplishments on a chart. In some classrooms, students have time in class to start their homework so that they can get extra help.

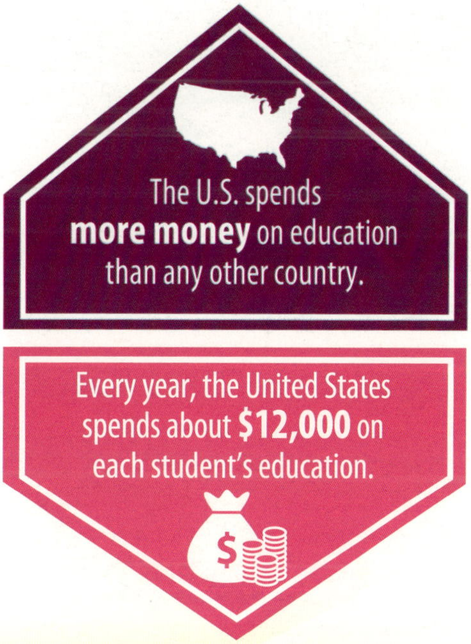

PRO

Some students feel motivated when they do homework with friends.

Homework Makes Students Better Learners

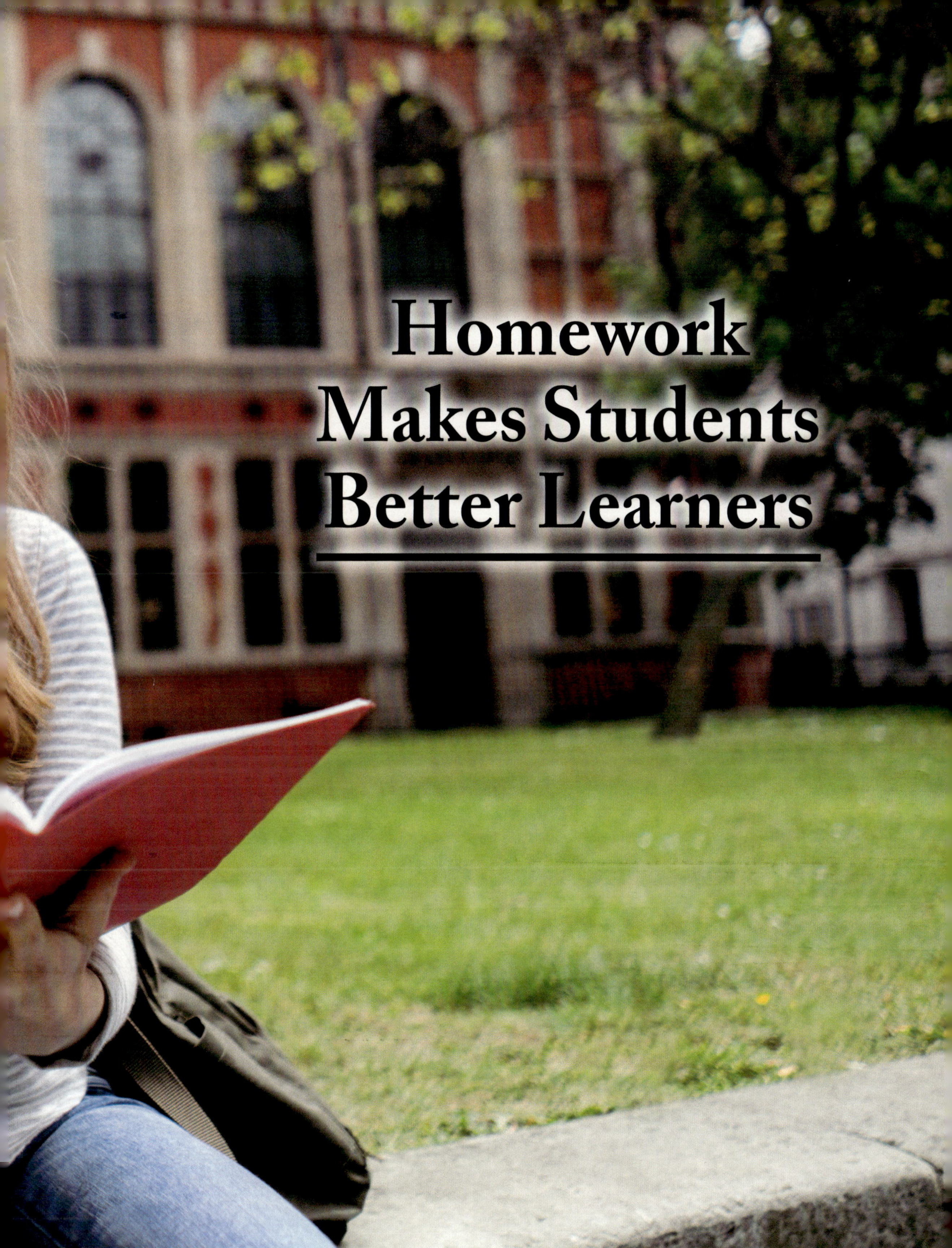

Strong study habits require focus and discipline.

Homework can lead to more than good grades. Many supporters of homework believe it makes students better learners. For example, when students do their homework and earn higher grades, their self-esteem improves. They learn that they achieve positive results when they work hard. They also learn that they are capable of doing the work. This helps increase their **intrinsic motivation**.

According to one study, homework also helps students develop strong study habits. When students get in the habit of doing homework, they become goal-focused. They may even develop a positive attitude toward their assignments. This sets them up for more school success in the future.

Those in favor of homework believe that regular homework also helps students learn **autonomy**. When students, instead of parents, are in charge of homework, they get better at completing it. Studies have shown that when students feel in control and responsible for assignments, they do better in class.

Balancing homework and activities such as sports helps students build responsibility.

Students have to make decisions about how to use their time. For instance, they may have to choose between sports, music lessons, homework, and spending time with friends. To learn how to make good decisions, students need practice. They get that practice by deciding when and where to do their homework. And when they choose not to do homework, they learn the consequences.

Holding students responsible for their homework teaches them how to manage their time and accept responsibility for their actions. This, in turn, helps students become better learners. When homework is a regular part of education, students are more likely to take learning seriously.

Good organizational skills help students succeed.

Good grades help students do well in school, but being a good learner can help a student develop skills for life. In 2014, researchers argued that skills in time management, communication, and decision-making help students become better learners. The researchers also included regular, consistent homework as one of the keys to increased learning.

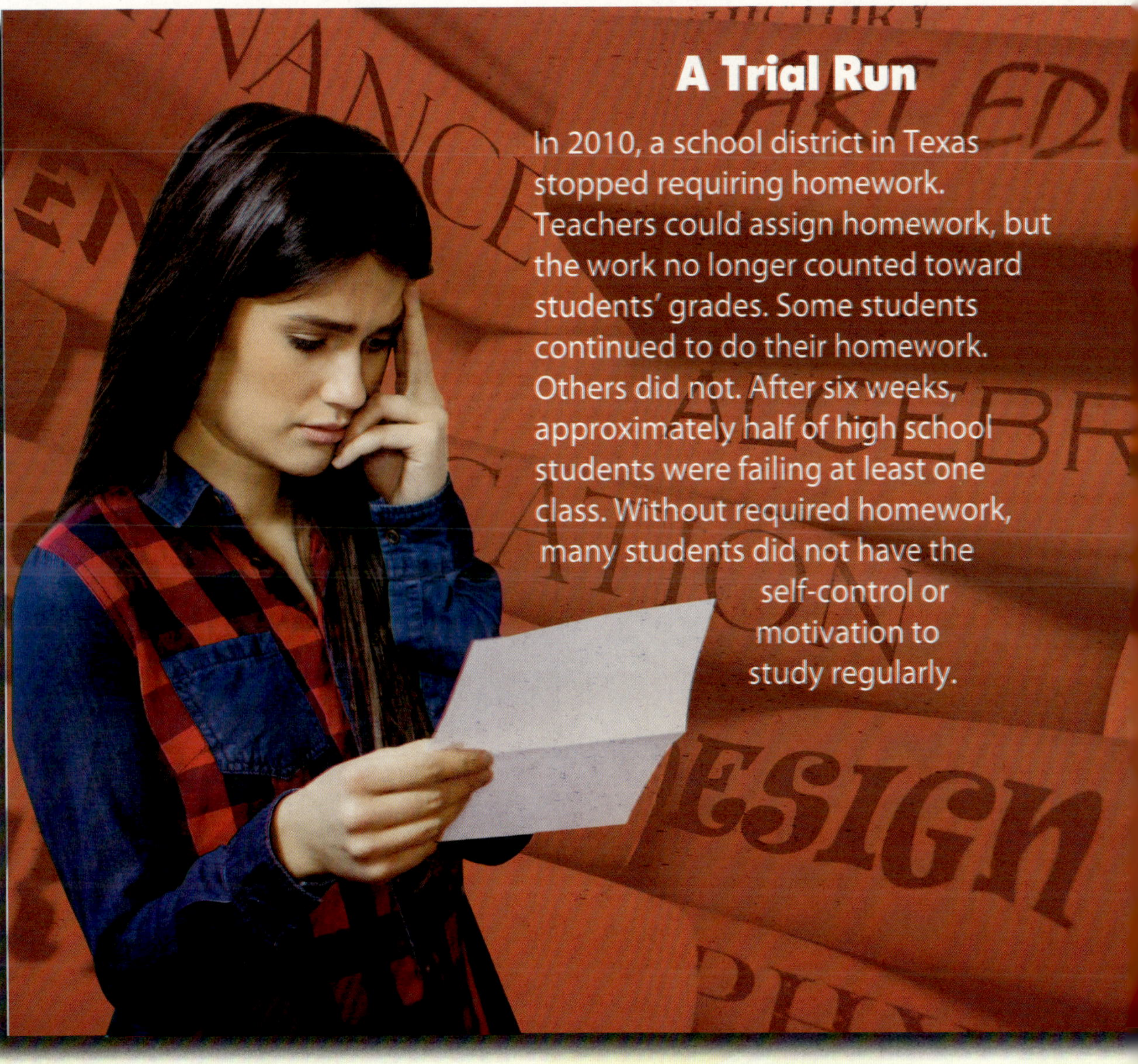

A Trial Run

In 2010, a school district in Texas stopped requiring homework. Teachers could assign homework, but the work no longer counted toward students' grades. Some students continued to do their homework. Others did not. After six weeks, approximately half of high school students were failing at least one class. Without required homework, many students did not have the self-control or motivation to study regularly.

PRO

Art homework strengthens the right side of the brain. Math homework strengthens the left.

Homework Is Good for the Brain

Just like the rest of the body, the brain needs exercise. When students do homework, they exercise their brains. They build important skills, such as how to pay attention, complete tasks, and remember details. By encouraging students to examine a topic more closely, homework helps them develop curious minds.

Homework positively affects the brain by increasing the time students spend on academics. Some schools lengthen the school day to increase students' time spent learning. Homework, however, is a more common method for extending learning time. That increased time, whether at school or after school, benefits students' brains.

Homework helps students become familiar with the material. This may increase their engagement in classroom activities.

Homework also benefits the brain by offering repeated practice of a skill. The brain learns by **repetition**. That is why babies do the same thing over and over. A baby who drops a spoon off a high chair 20 times learns about cause and effect. Each repetition creates new connections in the brain. These new connections are how a person learns new things. Completing multiple math problems may take time, but it trains the brain.

Learning something new is easiest when a student takes in small pieces of information over time. The brain is best at remembering information that is repeated and spaced out.

For example, manipulating fractions would be hard to learn all at once. Instead, a teacher will start by teaching students to add fractions. Then, they will move on to subtraction.

Students on school teams often practice sports after school. Repetition helps athletes improve their skill.

Taking in too much information at once can overwhelm the brain.

By the end of the week, students might learn to multiply and divide. In the evenings, students complete practice problems. This method gives the brain the best opportunity to learn.

Homework helps the brain grow through a process of trial and error. If one learning method does not work, students can try another. Effective homework presents material to students in a new way. For example, students might listen to a lesson on World War II in class. At night, they could read a book about a soldier's experience. Learning the subject in two different ways is good for the brain.

Similarly, students can use homework to expand their knowledge of things they learned in school. For example, students might build a birdhouse, plant a garden, or research a composer. These out-of-school experiences give students opportunities to learn in new ways. They also allow students to practice what they have learned. Homework does not always have to be a worksheet. When homework is designed well, it helps students form new connections in the brain.

Did You Know?

Science tells us that the brain can absorb only five to seven new pieces of information at a time.

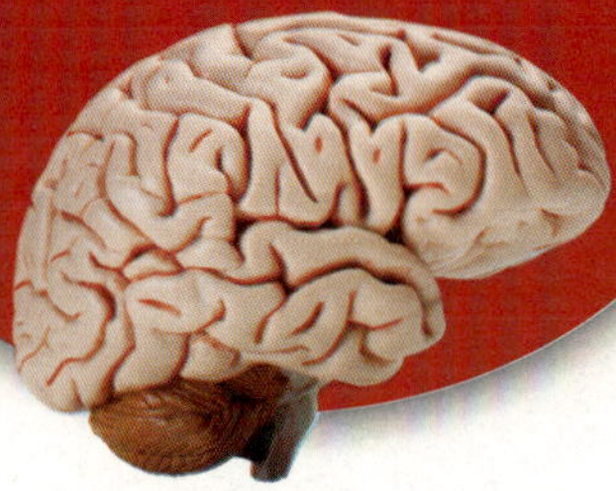

Music students learn by practicing their instrument and completing homework on music theory.

CON

School is not enjoyable for students who are stressed out.

Homework Leads to Unhealthy Stress

During the past few decades, homework amounts have increased across all grade levels. Students are assigned more and more homework at younger and younger ages. In 2007, U.S. high school students reported an average of more than two hours of homework per night.

This increase in homework causes students stress. Studies have shown that kids are more stressed out today than kids were in the 1950s. And today's students list homework as one of the top stressors in their lives.

Stress from homework can result in both physical and mental problems. Some students may have difficulty sleeping. Others may stay up all night trying to complete homework. To stay awake, some students use caffeine-filled drinks, such as coffee or soda. Similar to stress, too much caffeine can cause poor sleep, upset stomachs, and headaches.

Studies show that the more homework students have, the more they struggle with stress and other health problems. This includes tiredness, depression, anger, and **anxiety**. Research also shows that stress reduces the brain's ability to learn. When students are stressed, it is harder for them to remember what they learn. The brain functions best when it has periods of rest. A large amount of homework after a long day at school does not give students the break they need.

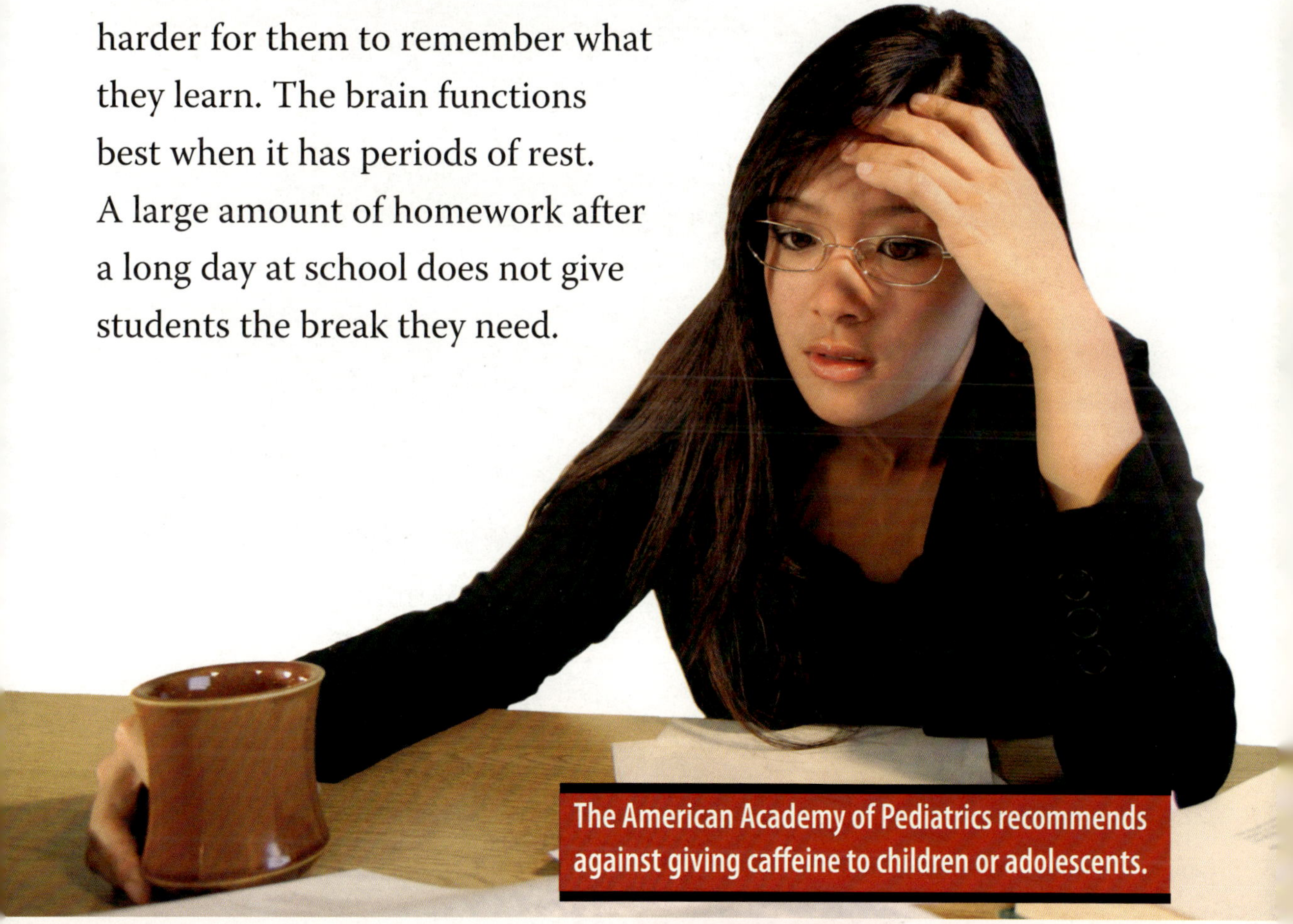

The American Academy of Pediatrics recommends against giving caffeine to children or adolescents.

Large amounts of homework can also put stress on students' relationships with their parents. Students often fight with their parents over homework. In some families, the only time parents talk to their children is to ask if their homework is complete. Parents and students who work on assignments together often argue as well. The more students struggle with homework, the more problems homework can cause in the family.

Families often fight when students procrastinate on their homework.

Requiring students to complete schoolwork at home can also be **inequitable**. Not all families can provide the same level of support for their children. Some parents might not have had much education, or the homework might be written in a language the parent does not know. In some cases, parents' work schedules might not allow them to be home during homework time. Access to technology is another example of inequality. Some students do not have the tools they need to do homework. They might not have a computer or internet connection at home.

For families who can help with homework, the help itself can be a problem. For example, parents might have learned to do math differently than their children. Some teachers have stopped assigning homework because parents show their children different ways to solve the problem. Teachers end up having to reteach the information. This can confuse students and cause teachers stress.

About 70 percent of U.S. teachers assign homework that requires internet access.

CON

Some students learn better in the classroom than they do at home.

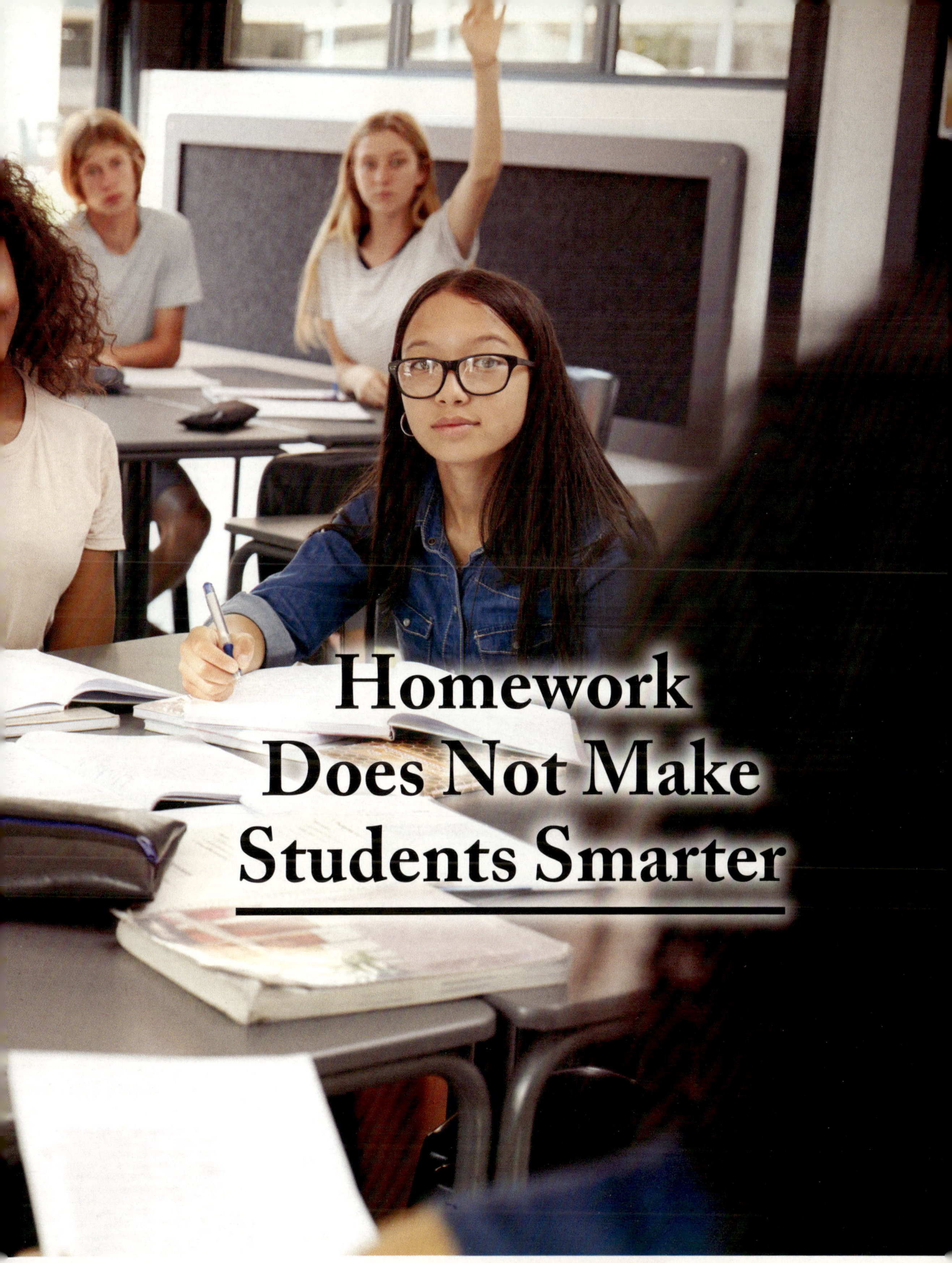

Homework Does Not Make Students Smarter

Some studies show an increase in academic achievement when students are given more homework. But others show that too much homework can have the opposite effect. For this reason, many educators are rethinking homework.

The benefits of homework are especially unclear for younger ages. One study found that the more homework elementary school students are assigned, the more their grades go down. Another study showed that children in elementary school do not do any better in school when they are assigned homework. When children have a lot of homework, they do not have as much time to play. Free time and play are an important part of brain development.

When young children play, they learn to make decisions and take risks.

The effects of homework vary for high school students. Some research has shown that large amounts of homework prevent high school students from getting enough sleep. Sleep is important for brain development, especially for teenagers. A different study tracked student performance through high school. Researchers found that students with less homework during their school careers were more likely to graduate.

Nearly one in five U.S. students will not graduate high school.

In some cases, homework can reduce students' desire to learn. Homework that is too difficult often causes frustration. Instead of learning the material, students develop negative attitudes toward it. Some students end up thinking they are not smart. These students' perceptions about homework prevent them from learning.

For other students, homework that is repetitive or long can be boring. Dozens of math problems testing the same skill might not be interesting to students who understand the material. They could be ready to move on to the next lesson. Repetitive homework offers useful practice. But it can also make students dislike learning.

The Flipped Classroom

Some teachers are flipping their classrooms. This means that work usually assigned as homework is done in class. And the material usually taught in class becomes homework. For most flipped classrooms, students are required to watch a video at home before the class period. The video or podcast teaches the information. At school, students work with their teacher and classmates on practicing the new material.

The problem can be much worse for children who do not understand their homework. For instance, practicing math problems will not help students if they have not learned the concept. These students will not be able to complete one problem, much less one hundred.

Students who are struggling may be tempted to cheat. Some students will attempt to hide what they do not know. This keeps them from learning the material. If students could spend more time on assignments in class, they would be more likely to get the help they need.

Cheating may help students get a good grade, but it does not help them learn.

1 in 3 U.S. high school students admits to using technology to **cheat**.

In 2017, more than **60** Harvard University students in a computer science course were suspected of cheating. They risked being **expelled**.

CON

Many high school students get a job so they can save for college. Others hope to build work experience.

Homework Limits Students' Other Interests

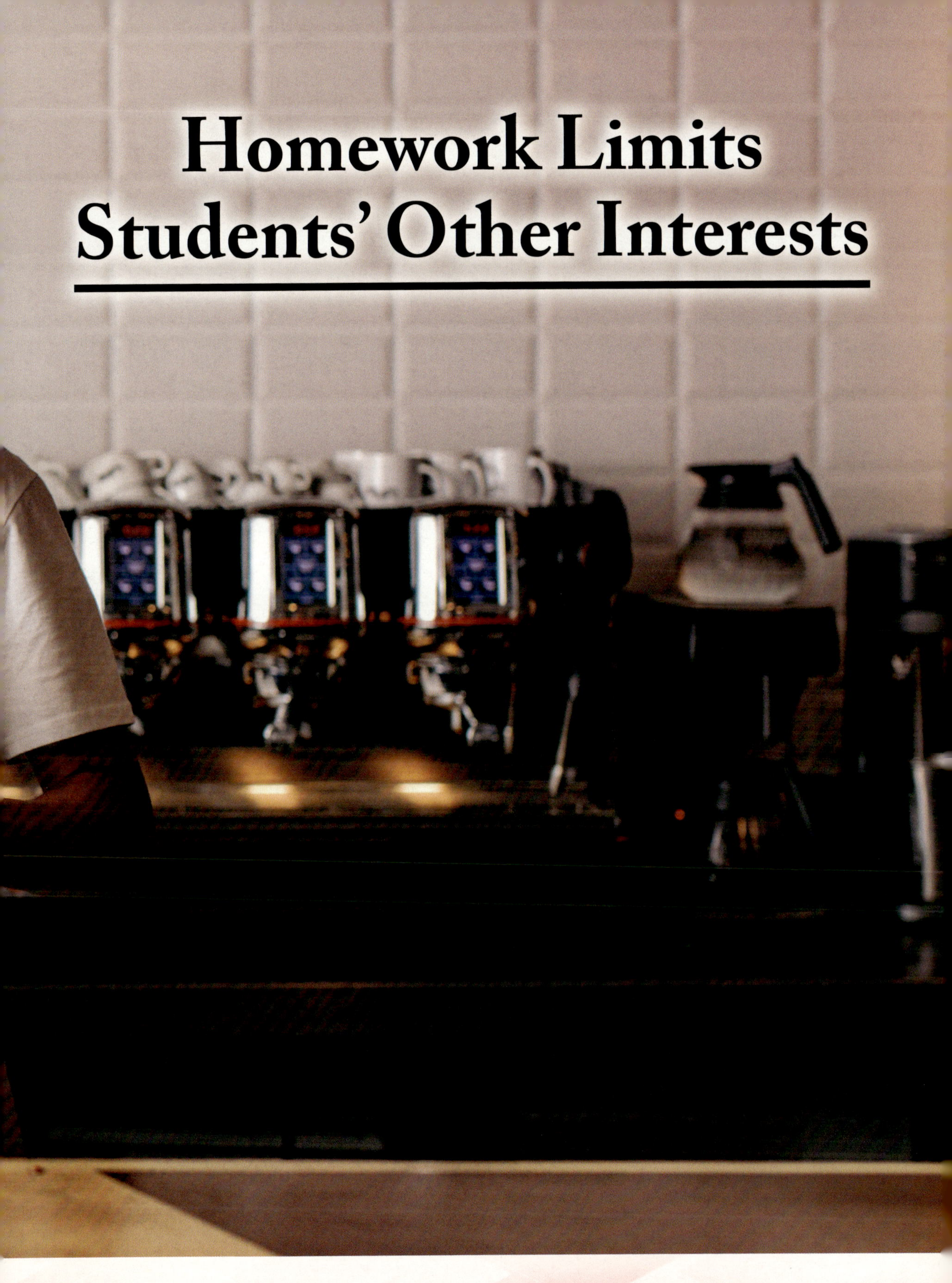

Family dinners can teach kids how to listen and hold a conversation.

Not all learning happens in a classroom or at a desk. Free time is just as likely to help kids learn. Without it, kids have fewer opportunities to develop non-academic skills. One example is family time. When students have large amounts of homework, they spend less time with family. Studies show that family time, such as eating together, is important. It can result in better grades and fewer behavior problems at school.

One benefit of family time is conversation. At dinner, students can discuss the highlights of their day. Or they can bring up problems they had at school. Dinnertime talk is also a learning opportunity. Students learn manners at the dinner table. They can also learn new vocabulary.

When students have hours of homework each night, they do not have time for activities such as sports or music. Hobbies help students broaden their interests. Some hobbies encourage students to set personal goals. Music students, for example, might strive to learn a difficult song. Homework also takes time away from fun activities and events with friends. These activities teach social skills, including sharing, compassion, and cooperation.

Hobbies can help students find careers they love.

Students might also have responsibilities or schedules that make it hard to complete hours of homework. Some students may need time at night to practice their religion. Others may need to babysit siblings or help with chores at home. Older students might have part-time jobs after school. Students should not have to decide between academic success and their other responsibilities.

Hours of homework also leave little time for **leisure** reading. In one survey, 22 percent of 13-year-olds reported that they never or hardly ever read for pleasure. Reading outside of school improves students' academic performance. It can also spark students' interest in topics not covered in school. Reading fiction can even help students build compassion toward others.

Activities outside of school also help students discover what they like to do. They might learn how to bake a cake or build a skate ramp. By learning new things, kids build passions and talents. They may start to consider future careers.

Pros and Cons Summary

PROS

- Homework makes it harder for students to procrastinate.
- Homework helps students learn new concepts, practice skills, and prepare for exams.
- Some studies show that doing homework can improve students' grades and test scores.
- Regularly assigned homework teaches students responsibility and time management skills.
- Homework provides opportunities for learning beyond the classroom.
- Homework helps the brain grow and create new connections.

CONS

- Stress about homework can weaken students' physical and mental health.
- Homework affects households by taking away family time and placing strain on relationships.
- Homework is unfair to families who are unable to provide students with homework support.
- Too much homework can lead students to dislike both homework and learning.
- Too much homework can prevent kids from building non-academic passions and interests.
- Spending hours on homework leaves little time for students to develop social skills.

Homework Map

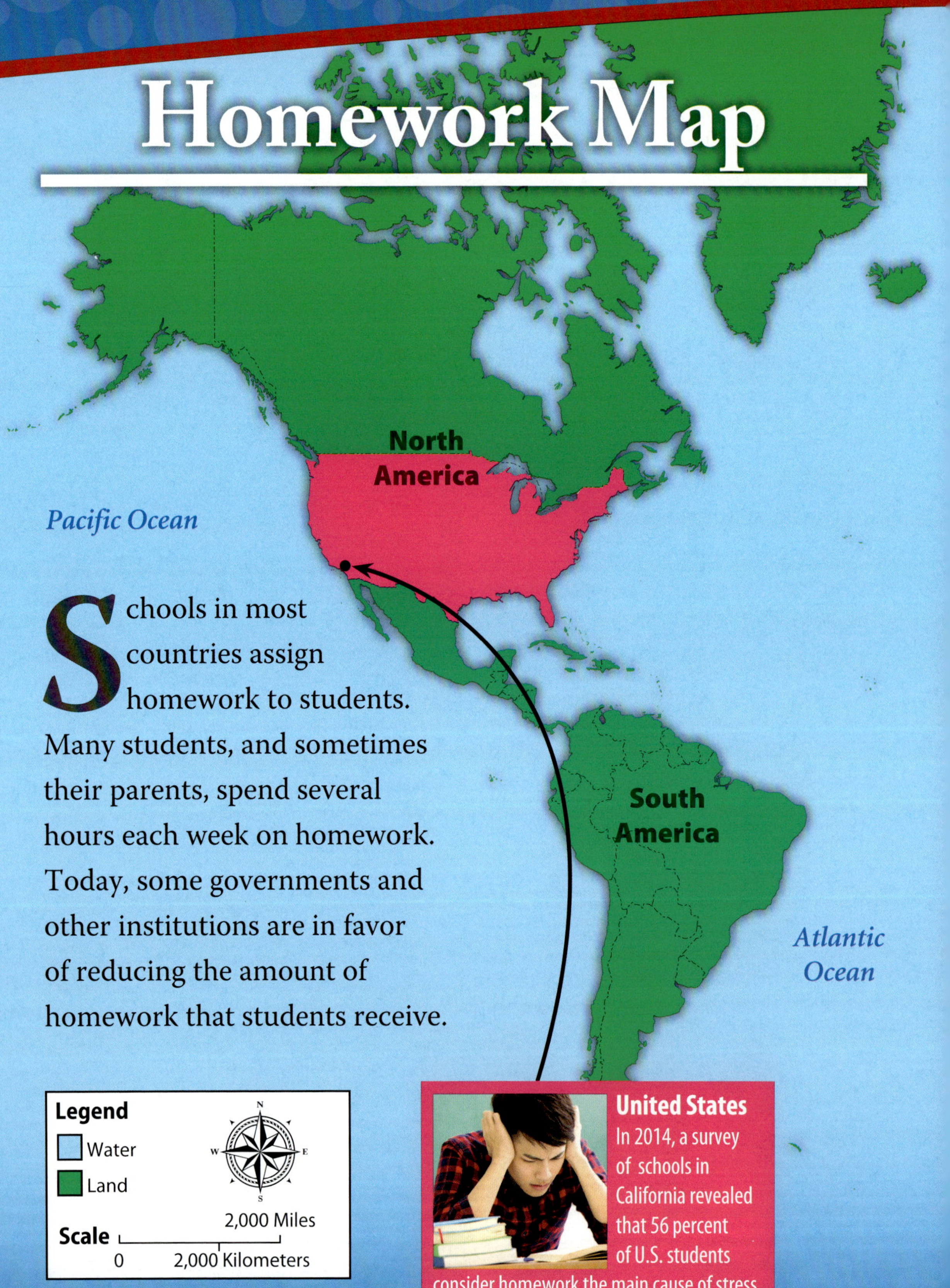

Schools in most countries assign homework to students. Many students, and sometimes their parents, spend several hours each week on homework. Today, some governments and other institutions are in favor of reducing the amount of homework that students receive.

United States
In 2014, a survey of schools in California revealed that 56 percent of U.S. students consider homework the main cause of stress in their lives.

France In 2012, in a speech at Sorbonne University in Paris, former French President Francois Hollande promised to ban homework in French elementary and middle schools.

China In 2013, the Chinese Ministry of Education in Beijing released a guideline against assigning written homework to students in elementary school.

India In 2018, the Madras High Court in Chennai banned a majority of Indian schools from assigning homework to Grade 1 and 2 students.

Quiz

1 When did the U.S. Congress create a law to support standardized testing?

2 Which subject is most commonly assigned as homework?

3 What non-academic skills does homework teach students?

4 Which side of the brain does art homework strengthen?

5 How many new pieces of information can the brain absorb at a time?

6 What kind of health problems can too much homework cause?

7 What is a flipped classroom?

8 In which country do students younger than 13 rarely have homework?

ANSWERS **1.** The early 2000s **2.** Math **3.** Responsibility and time management **4.** Right side **5.** Five to seven **6.** Stress, tiredness, depression, anger, and anxiety **7.** In flipped classrooms, work usually assigned as homework is done in class, while material generally taught in class becomes homework **8.** Finland

Key Words

academic: having to do with school or school work

anxiety: a feeling of extreme worry or nervousness

autonomy: the freedom to make decisions and take on responsibility

Cold War: the politically tense relationship between the United States and the Soviet Union after World War II

correlation: a relationship between one thing and another

inequitable: unfair or not equal

intrinsic motivation: a desire to act that is based on personal goals instead of rewards given by other people

leisure: free time

PISA: the Programme for International Student Assessment (PISA) is a worldwide survey that tests fifteen-year-olds on a range of subjects

procrastinate: to put off doing something

repetition: doing something over and over

standardized testing: tests that are designed to compare students' knowledge and skill levels

Index

Dewey, John 5

education 13, 18, 31, 45
elementary school 34, 45

family 30, 40, 41, 43
Finland 6, 7, 42, 46

grades 8, 9, 10, 11, 12, 16, 19, 34, 37, 40, 43

high school 19, 28, 35, 37, 38

math 5, 6, 11, 12, 20, 23, 31, 36, 37, 46
memorization 5, 12

repetition 7, 23, 36
research 5, 10, 11, 19, 25, 29, 35

skills 12, 18, 19, 22, 23, 36, 40, 41, 43, 46
stress 26, 27, 28, 29, 30, 31, 43, 44, 46

Log on to www.av2books.com

AV² by Weigl brings you media enhanced books that support active learning. Go to www.av2books.com, and enter the special code found on page 2 of this book. You will gain access to enriched and enhanced content that supplements and complements this book. Content includes video, audio, weblinks, quizzes, a slide show, and activities.

AV² Online Navigation

Audio
Listen to sections of the book read aloud

Book Pages
AV² pages directly correspond to pages in the book.

Video
Watch informative video clips.

Embedded Weblinks
Gain additional information for research.

Key Words
Study vocabulary, and complete a matching word activity.

Try This!
Complete activities and hands-on experiments.

Quizzes
Test your knowledge.

Slide Show
View images and captions, and prepare a presentation.

AV² was built to bridge the gap between print and digital. We encourage you to tell us what you like and what you want to see in the future.

Sign up to be an AV² Ambassador at www.av2books.com/ambassador.

Due to the dynamic nature of the Internet, some of the URLs and activities provided as part of AV² by Weigl may have changed or ceased to exist. AV² by Weigl accepts no responsibility for any such changes. All media enhanced books are regularly monitored to update addresses and sites in a timely manner. Contact AV² by Weigl at 1-866-649-3445 or av2books@weigl.com with any questions, comments, or feedback.